Kelly Wilson's The Art of Seduction
Nine Easy Ways to Get Sex From Your Mate

Kelly Wilson

Table of Contents

Author's Notes, aka Reader Beware

Guess what? This is not a legitimate sex book. It is a satire.

I offer apologies in advance to readers who will read through this guide and try some of the strategies. While some may work – because even monkeys will type coherent sentences once in awhile - many readers will fail miserably at getting the desired sexual results.

When I told my husband that I was writing this little gem, his exact words were, "Dear God, woman, leave me out of this one." I am happy to report that all of the strategies included in this non-legitimate sex satire are based on words that I – the author – have actually said to my husband at one time or another.

My husband and I married when I was twenty, and I simply did not have much of a sex drive. Then I turned thirty, and my hormones exploded. All bets were off.

My sex drive has been off the charts for several years now, and it turns out that I have always been and continue to be terrible at getting the sex I need. Every time I told my closest friends about the latest failed sexual encounter with Husband, I would write it down at the encouragement of one friend in particular, eventually forming the foundation of this little guide.

How I try to get sex from Husband continues to be simply awful, but remains vastly entertaining. And sometimes he has mercy on me anyway, so maybe these strategies are not as terrible as they might seem.

Onward and the best of luck!

Introduction

What's the point of marriage if not to get sex whenever you need it?

True, years of mind-numbing routine and the presence of children will ruin the mood for even the horniest man or woman. Every day we get up, get dressed (this may be our first mistake when it comes to getting more sex), work all day, raise kids, and try to decide for the fifteen-thousandth time how to cook that pound of hamburger meat so that family members will happily eat it without complaining. And there's nothing like having to clean up puke in the middle of the night or one of your kids decorating a wall of your home with poop to kill a sexy vibe.

Sometimes even the most vivid memory of the best orgasm that happened that one time isn't enough to produce the required loin spark to move from the comfy couch, much less convince a couple to actually undress and then participate in coital hijinks.

While I understand the countless ways that regular, humdrum, ordinary life can kill the desire and opportunity for sexual encounters, my libido rears its energetic head several times a week. This pattern of wanting to do my husband, Louis C.K., and Wolverine (not at the same time) started on my 30th birthday and hasn't slowed down since.

The burning of my late-blooming loin fire has created tension – much of it unpleasant – in my marriage because my spousal partner isn't a machine created to coddle my every whim. This proved to be a surprise.

So instead of fighting about getting the sex I needed fairly frequently, I came up with this guide of wisdom in the hope that spouses and significant others everywhere don't suffer as I have over the last several years. These artful seduction ideas are presented on "The Spectrum of Sexual Persuasion," which begins with the more passive aggressive "Calling the Waiter" and ends with "The Threat of Death."

Simply choose the technique you feel best fits with your situation, and get ready to either have sex or fight about it!

11

Spectrum Of Sexual Persuasion

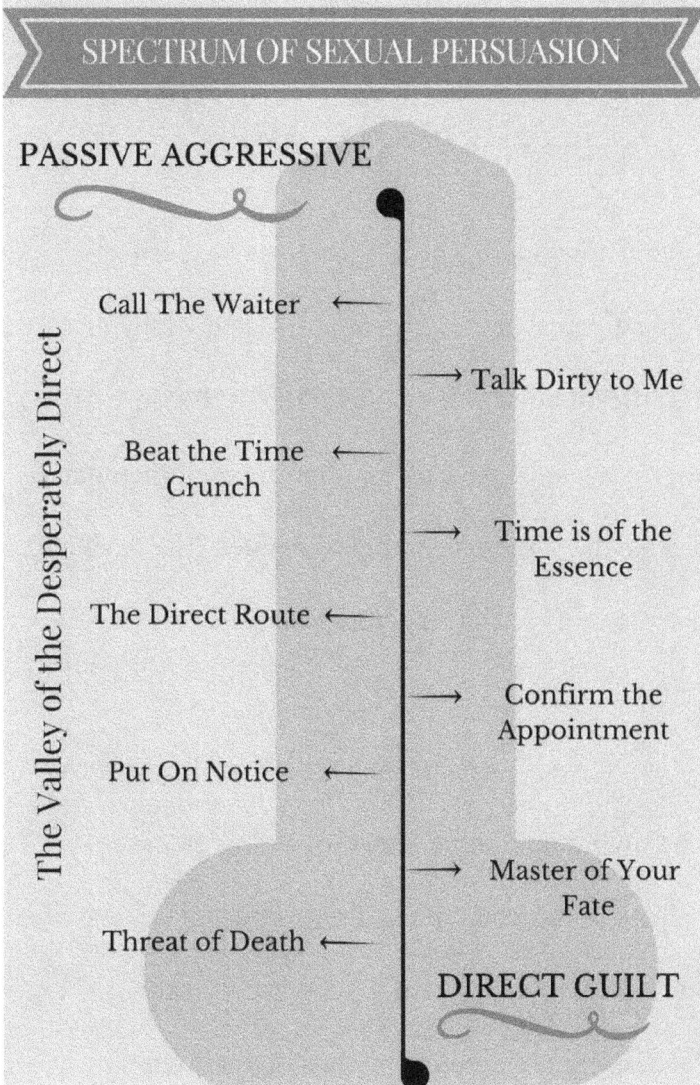

SPECTRUM OF SEXUAL PERSUASION

PASSIVE AGGRESSIVE

Call The Waiter ←

→ Talk Dirty to Me

Beat the Time ←
Crunch

→ Time is of the
Essence

The Direct Route ←

→ Confirm the
Appointment

Put On Notice ←

→ Master of Your
Fate

Threat of Death ←

DIRECT GUILT

The Valley of the Desperately Direct

Technique #1: Calling the Waiter

Imagine sitting in your favorite, even romantic, restaurant. You are on a date with your significant other without the children. Because of the tightness of your pants, your meals throughout the day have consisted of coffee, three Ritz crackers, a scrap of a banana, and your youngest child's leftover yogurt.

Leaving behind the high chair, dirty dishes and nighttime routine, you are joining the rest of society during the typical dinner hour for the rest of the world, as opposed to 4:30, when you are used to feeding the children to simply stop their whining.

The result is waiting for about 30 minutes for a table after you have already hunted for a pair of pants that don't start with the term "yoga" and a shirt that is clean but not too wrinkled to require the use of something called an iron, which is an appliance that you are sure you once had but can no longer locate in your home.

The server who doesn't seem to actually be responsible for anything in particular has brought you water, which in your desperation for sustenance you chugged like a pirate after a three hour separation from rum. And the waiter still has not appeared.

Or worse, he appeared once to check on you, but has not reappeared to actually take your order and get the food onto the table and into your digestive system where it will bring immeasurable comfort and feelings of happiness.

At this point, the thought might cross your mind, "Hey, what does it take to get a little service around here?"

This is a fair question, especially when it comes to food…and your sexual needs. Perhaps it's been days or weeks since your last carnal encounter of any kind. Maybe you have been waiting at the table of sexual dissatisfaction and you just need a little investment of time and attention to achieve the endorphin action in your brain that helps make life worth living.

It's time to Call the Waiter.

Since this is one end of *The Spectrum of Sexual Persuasion,* this is a fairly passive and even humorous technique to get the sex you need from your mate. Here are the steps:

1. Check to ensure that you are alone, or at least make sure the children won't hear you unless you decide that, in fact, this is the perfect time for an uncomfortable discussion regarding what you are about to say and what that has to do with sex.

2. Clear your throat and adopt a smirk, which is basically a lazy, close-mouthed smile that halfway approaches a frown. It says, "My facial expression doesn't match my tone. Be aware that this conversation can go south pretty quick."

3. For a more casual bent, say, "Hey, what's it take for a girl to get serviced around here?"[1]

---

[1] Obviously if you are male, change the "girl" to "guy" or "dude" or "bruh" or "bro," or prepare to have a confusing and potentially tense conversation regarding why you are calling yourself a girl and haven't done so before now.

For a more formal and serious tone, drop the "Hey," raise your voice in pitch so that it is a shrill and demanding cry, and enunciate, "What does it take for a girl to get serviced around here?"

"By the Way" will work instead of "Hey" for the casual tone, and even resembles a joke in that your partner is going to think that you mean to remind him or her about routine business of the household and instead, there is a surprising and delightful ending.

Which is what we are all hoping for when using this technique.

4. Don't forget the importance of facial expressions to communicate intensity or desire. Close your eyes halfway and invest in more of a smile instead of a smirk to make this technique more persuasive. Keep in

mind not to close your eyes too much, as you'll just look drunk or tired, and this will help nobody.

However, if you've been waiting at the table of sexual frustration for a long time, then flaring the nostrils, widening your eyes and gritting your teeth like a bull ready to charge can help convey your displeasure in the lack of service you have received at this establishment without ever having to say a word.

It is entirely possible that the waiter will be unresponsive. If that's the case, consider a more aggressive technique in this Art of Seduction.

Or maybe just stop cooking dinner. That might work too.

Technique #2: Talk Dirty To Me

Oral sex, while enjoyable in the traditional sense, doesn't all happen south of the border. A significant amount of foreplay can occur through simple interaction, orally through the spoken words, using facial expressions, and employing certain hand gestures. The following suggestions can help partners communicate their sexual needs to each other in persuasive ways that can still be fun.

Simply Ask

This is a powerful technique that is both deceptively simple and incredibly uncomfortable. While nobody can know your secret wishes and dreams, it can still be awkward to just come right out and ask for sex. These delicate phrases may help get the idea across without leaving the asker too vulnerable to rejection.

- "Wanna do a little sumpin'-sumpin'?"
- "Are we gonna do it or not?"
- "So…what about the sex?"
- "Want to pay the bills? Or do some Bible Study? How about finishing that paperwork?"

The last one is clearly using code phrases. Be aware that this practice can be risky. First, you and your partner should decide on a specific code phrase before you try this exercise in order to avoid confusion, as she or he may think that you actually want to participate in these non-sexy tasks. A misunderstanding will inevitably lead to additional explanations, and conversation isn't what you're looking for at this point. Plus, should the kids knock on the door, you can call out that you're in the middle of Bible Study and will be out in awhile. Win-win!

Facial Expressions

It is important to acknowledge the power of a facial expression. Using the 50 muscles of the face, you can make thousands of facial expressions. It's time to work those facial muscles to get the sex that we need!

Use your facial expressions to your advantage by creating a *Sex Face*. This set expression can be used again and again to communicate to your partner that it's time to get it on without the threat of anyone eavesdropping.

While you will need to devise your own *Sex Face*, here's an example of one to begin with. Tested over time, this facial expression never fails to communicate the passion and desire to "do some bible study."

- Start with eyes half-closed, making eyelids heavy
- Tense the eyebrow muscles, making your eyes kind of squinty
- Jut out the lower jaw so that there's an extreme underbite
- Tense the muscles of the lower jaw and the upper neck, exposing the bottom teeth. Leave the upper lip covering the top teeth

Here is a helpful photo illustration of the *Sex Face*.

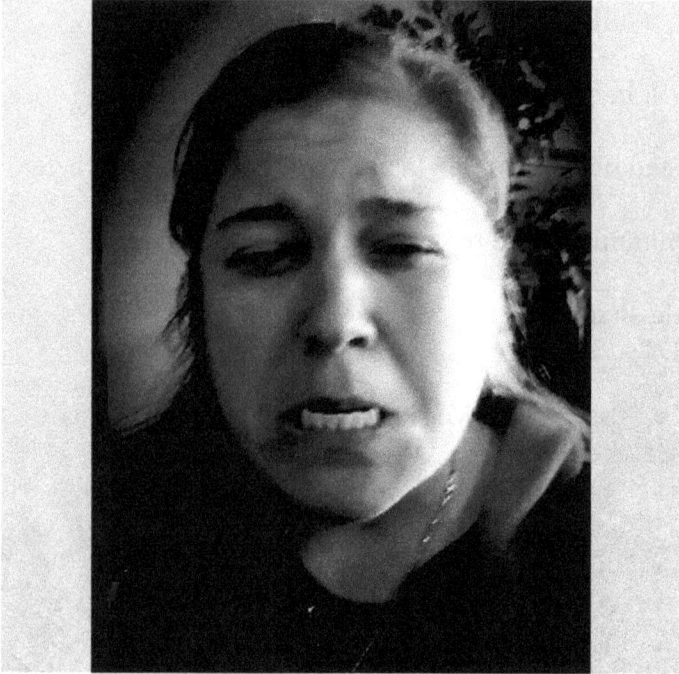

The Sex Face is nothing without the accompanying noise, which is halfway between a donkey's bray and the sound of a Sasquatch pooping in the woods. The breathy moan combined with the acerbic wail is sure to communicate your sexual prowess and desire to your partner without ever having to utter an actual recognizable word.

Readers should not feel limited to this one example of the *Sex Face* – make it your own! Another variation of the *Sex Face* mimics a popular selfie pose, in which the lips are pursed like a duck. With eyes squinted and lips plumped and ducked out, you can then pulse the lips ever so slightly. This technique wouldn't be complete without the requisite licking of the lips, opening the mouth and running the tongue around the surface of the lips until you start to drool and/or your mouth dries out.

Crude Hand Gestures

This form of communication is not just for junior high kids. A well-timed hand gesture can communicate the depths of your need with the added benefit of complete silence. Plus, hand gestures can be given across a crowded room, behind the backs of nosy children, and while driving in the car, among other places.

One particularly helpful hand gesture that leaves no room for misinterpretation is the Finger-Through-The-Hole scenario. Close one hand almost into a fist, and leave a small space in the shape of a circle, big enough to look through. Take the pointer finger of the other hand and poke it through this round space. If the space is enclosed enough, there should be a rasping sound when the finger is moved back and forth through the hole.

While crude, this hand gesture is surprisingly elegant in its simplicity, and leaves no room for confusion regarding what the gesturer could possible mean. These clear and subtle communication tools might be just what you need to get your sexual

needs met.

These particular strategies are not technically

oral, but they incorporate levels of communication

to help partners play show and tell regarding urgent

sexual needs.

Technique #3: Beating the Time Crunch

Time is the murderer of sex.

If you are an adult who participates in life, you will feel tired and just not into the idea of actually taking off your clothes, kissing, caressing, and generally taking the time required for a stereotypically satisfying sexual experience.

At the end of a long day, sometimes you just want to recline in a fluffy chair in sweatpants with a bucket of fried chicken in your lap and a bottle of wine within easy reach. Not remotely sexy, but the obligations and commitments of everyday life – the commute, the job, the kids, the mountains of laundry, the grocery shopping, the endless meal preparations - can grind the sexiness right out of the most well-meaning, previously horny person.

The conflict occurs when the fatigue of life combined with the time it takes to have sex isn't enough to thoroughly kill the urge. A pocket of warmth gathers in the loin region, awakening desire that, like a cranky baby, will not be ignored no matter how tired you happen to be.

There is, however, a way to get the satisfaction needed without requiring a lot of time. Taken at its most basic level, sex is for reproductive purposes during which sperm travels up to an egg that needs fertilization. Performed as such, this act can take as little as 30 seconds if the conditions are ripe.

But for those of us either not interested in reproduction and/or simply chasing the pleasure of the non-caloric source of dopamine that sex provides, we can forget that having sex doesn't have to take very long at all.

This strategy – Beating the Time Crunch - is all about operating within an agreed-upon Scope of Minimum Expectations. The exact scope can be predetermined beforehand or decided during what would usually constitute the act of foreplay, as indicated in the following chart.

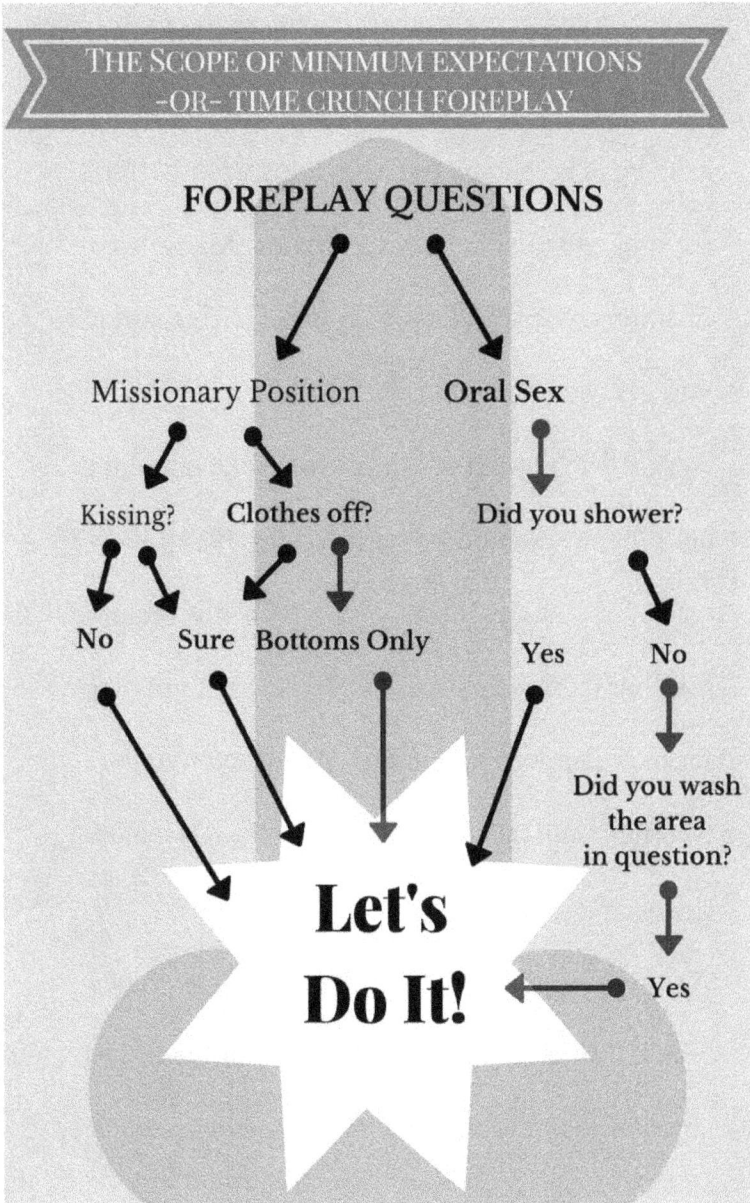

As seen in the chart, there are basically two types of sex available when there is a lack of time, as there is no energy to either think of or perform anything approaching creativity: the Missionary Position or Oral Sex. Keep it simple. This will help you get what you want.

The second consideration is the amount of clothing that should be removed for this strategy to work. Take off as little – or as much – as required for your particular situation. The easiest option by far is to remove the bottoms of whatever you are wearing, but feel free to keep the rest on (including socks).

And the third element of this abbreviated brand of foreplay involves basic cleanliness. The chart leaves room for lack of kissing in case one or both of you wants to avoid teeth brushing. However, the cleaning of the groinal regions is as good as required. Even while in a hurry, nobody wants to deal with nut cheese. This material is sometimes known as "Fromundah Cheese," as it is like "toe jam," only much grosser, and is located From Undah The Ball Sac. Pass a soapy washcloth over the area and rinse with water. Your partner will - quite literally and out loud - thank you.

On the Spectrum of Sexual Persuasion, this strategy is the first to occur in The Valley of the Desperately Direct. Remember that the loins are already throbbing, ready to go, making the situation ideal for skipping foreplay altogether. This allows you to enjoy a more honest approach, so blunt as to verge on rudeness. Stand up straight, roll the shoulders back, look your partner in the eye, and state clearly, "Just do me for five minutes. It's probably not going to take that long.

Once your partner realizes that, in fact, having sex with the *Scope of Minimum Expectations* can be both quick and simple, the problem might be solved and you can go at it for the five minutes or so that it will take. However, your partner might need more persuasion, like a reminder that you are not, in fact, taking out the trash and that sex does, in fact, feel pretty good. Both of you will benefit from Beating the Time Crunch, especially using the aforementioned chart, which can help persuade your partner to give you some lovin' with just a hint of gentle direct communication.

Technique #4: Time is of the Essence –or– Just Give Me the Enchilada

The previous strategy – *Beating the Time Crunch* - dealt with a perceived lack of time to actually have sex and referred primarily to foreplay. This strategy, called Time is of the Essence, deals with what is traditionally known as The Afterglow, in which satisfied post-coital participants shared a cigarette in the movies and TV shows of the 1970s and 1980s.

There are times when partners just want to have sex without the usual trappings of activities like talking and snuggling. Consider for a moment a strong desire for a cheese enchilada. You sit down in a Mexican restaurant, and because you don't want the rice and beans that come with the Grande Combination plate, you simply order an enchilada ala carte. Then you eat the enchilada and are completely satisfied, not missing the rice and beans at all.

This was not a personal affront to said rice and beans, you just weren't in the mood for them. You merely wanted to eat a bunch of cheese enrobed in a corn tortilla and covered in a blanket of red sauce.

In our busy, hectic lives full of obligations and commitments, the idea of sitting down to a Grande Combination plate of sex with our partners can be simply too overwhelming to consider. First talk with your partner about the idea of "Just Give Me the Enchilada." If you and your partner agree that foregoing the "rice and beans" of the Afterglow is acceptable at exceptionally busy times, there are a couple of phrases that can help set these boundaries to save both time and energy.

The Poke-n-Go

Perhaps you have brought up the idea of having sex with your partner, and he or she simply is not into it. It's been a crazy day, the kids are sick, there are several evening commitments during the week, or work has been incredibly stressful.

To remind your partner of your agreement to simply "Just Give Me the Enchilada," ask him or her if there is interest in The Poke-n-Go.

The Poke-n-Go practice of having sex is quite literal in its meaning. There is a series of poking with the appropriate body parts or apparatus and then…that's it. No snuggling, no conversation, no lolling about letting your heart rate slow down, no cigarette smoking.

Just put your clothes on and get on with life, probably feeling a lot calmer and with a smile on your face.

A very important reminder: this strategy **must** be reviewed and agreed up by both partners **before use**. The author takes absolutely no responsibility for people who disregard this important communication tip and leave partners without the anticipated rice and beans. Should readers then have to sleep on the couch, the author states, "Hey, that's on you."

The Poke-n-Stay

The Poke-n-Stay is a fun alternative to the Poke-n-Go; in other words, the Poke-n-Stay is the enchilada with the rice and beans. The Poke-n-Stay is also quite literal. There is poking of the appropriate parts, and then there is time to enjoy the Afterglow.

Once the poking is finished, there is no need to rush off. Stay to appreciate each other's performances, express gratitude, have some water, watch a show while snuggling, and – of course – share a cigarette if both parties are amenable.

One of the major advantages of this strategy is that it works well for partners who have children.

Either the Poke-n-Go or the Poke-n-Stay can be completed within the time it takes for children of all ages to watch a favorite television program. Plus, this strategy is ripe for being able to use coded language in front of the children.

For example, one person could comment that he or she is in the mood for an enchilada. The partner in the relationship needs only to ask, "A la carte? Or rice and beans?" Children will think that their parents are referring to their dinner plans, when actually they are planning something endlessly more fun and satisfying than the evening meal.

The point is that both partners can negotiate on a Poke-n-Go or Poke-n-Stay before heading into the bedroom while not alerting others to their perfect plans. This agreement provides each person with clear expectations of how the encounter will fit into their busy lives, whether enjoying the enchilada ala carte, or with rice and beans.

Technique #5: The Direct Route

Sexual frustration is stressful both physically and emotionally. Someone truly in need of sex considers leaning against the washer on spin cycle or turning her phone to the highest vibrate setting. The massage chair with the vibration in the seat at the nail salon also appears to be a pretty good alternative.

That, my friends, is desperation.

Desperate for sex is also what women have described as the feeling of just wanting their partners to lie on top of them. There is actually something very comforting about having somebody drape himself over you like a blanket. This is a very effective way to transfer heat, and can be helpful during cold winter months, especially if your chosen partner has a lot of body hair.

Even though this strategy is nestled smack in the center of the *Valley of the Desperately Direct* on *The Spectrum of Sexual Persuasion*, being direct does not mean being rude. Believe me, there's a time and place for rudeness, and I will cover those opportunities later in this guide.

"Being direct" simply means to be blunt and to the point. Like a penis, in fact. And the more creative you can be while directly asking for sex, the better. This allows you to directly communicate what you need in a more comfortable atmosphere. Being creative makes it far less likely that your partner will refuse your request. Plus, you'll be so entertaining that your partner will be simply too amused to turn you down.

Channel some of that sexually frustrated energy into using one or more of these creatively direct methods to ask for the sex you need.

Verbally

This is akin to begging; but remember, you are desperate enough to be as direct as possible. Simply approach your partner and say, "Please, for the love of all that is holy, have sex with me."

This is the most direct route, and needs to be employed with a large measure of sincerity so as to extract as much sympathy – and yes, pity – as possible. Refer to *the Poke-n-Go* and/or *Beating the Time Crunch* if necessary for the purpose of persuasion, as both of those aforementioned strategies get to the point of what you need quickly and without any unnecessary frills, like conversation or snuggling. You can get that stuff later.

Spiritually

If there was ever a time to invite your partner to have some Bible Study, that time is now. Remember, "Bible Study" is code for coital hijinks, and serves to preserve your children's innocence. Plus, if you adopt this code often, they will think you are spiritually wise, what with all of that study. Refer to *Talk Dirty to Me* for more information on successfully using this technique.

Textually

Smartphones make it really easy for partners to send sexual signals without verbally saying anything. Texting your partner is ideal when it comes to asking for sex from your mate, especially when using code words such as Give Me the Enchilada, Poke-n-Go, and Poke-n-Stay.

While code words are not necessary in asking for the sex that you need, they are recommended. It is important for partners to remember that nothing is private anymore, including any words or photos that may be texted back and forth. Even if you've deleted texts and photos that have turned into sexting, those steamy bits are still stored on a server somewhere. This author recommends texting code words that nobody else will understand; you only need your partner to respond to your text, after all.

Hypothermially

If you're a lady, remove your bra and huck your shirt up over your boobs. The armpit and sideboob fat will hold the fabric in place. Then walk around the house and ask your partner, "Hey, is it cold in here? I might get hypothermia." Wait for a response from your partner, such as surprise or chuckling, and then say, "Hey, since my shirt is basically off, we should have sex now."

If you're a dude, undo your britches and nestle the material around your sac so you can show off your goods (a hair trim wouldn't hurt either, by the way, along with a quick wash and rinse). Then walk around the house and ask your partner, "Hey, is it cold in here? I might get hypothermia." Wait for a response from your partner, such as surprise or chuckling, and then announce, "Hey, Hey, since my underwear is basically off, we should have sex now."

Musically

Hook up the mp3 player and blast Nelly's song that states, "It's getting hot in here / so take off all your clothes." Then, take off all your clothes and start dancing. Play the song until your partner arrives to find out what's going on, and then announce, "I'm hot, and look, I'm already naked! Let's have sex right now."

Edibly

They say the way to a man's heart is through his stomach. I'm not a man, but I love me some food, too. Why not use food to help tempt your mate into having sex?

There are several foods that can be considered "sexy" or "romantic." Champagne is a romantic way to help relax your partner and put him or her in the mood, what with all of those suggestive bubbles. Foods that are known as proven aphrodisiacs include oysters, avocado, chili peppers, chocolate, and, ironically, bananas.

Frisky partners can also consider wearing their food in order to encourage sexual encounters. A standby move in this arena is to apply whipped cream as a covering for your intimate nubbins. For example, a woman may spray this delicious topping over her breasts and nether region, appearing as if she were wearing a bikini made of whipped cream that could ostensibly be removed by the application of her partner's mouth. Individuals interested in edible products are only limited by their imaginations and food intolerances.

Any food allergies or intolerances are to be taken seriously, and partners should be well versed on one another's food issues. For example, I am extremely intolerant to dairy and cane sugar, so the whole whipped cream idea would send me into an insulin-resistant, diarrheal spin that is decidedly unsexy. Not to mention those individuals who are (ironically) allergic to nuts, who could die simply from trying to be sexy. The author recommends full knowledge of food issues before bringing tragedy into the bedroom.

Subliminally

While an argument could be made that a subliminal strategy is not necessarily direct, the fact is that the word "sex" will be used several times in the course of a conversation. You simply cannot get more direct than by saying the word "sex" to your partner several times in a row.

Start a conversation with your partner, interjecting the word "sex" every three or four words. For example:

"Hi, honey, how was (sex) your day? You look great (sex)."

The amount of times you include the word "sex" is an art, not a science! Keep a calm, straight face and act like you're having an ordinary conversation. For this to be truly subliminal, the word "sex" doesn't need to be shouted, just stated quietly in the rhythm of the sentence. This might take some practice, but it will then be a strategy you can easily whip out and use when truly desperate.

There are many creative ways that we can directly ask our partners for sex while drastically reducing the risk of rejection. Remember, the more creative, the better!

Technique #6: Setting and Keeping the Appointment

This is one of the more sane strategies in the *Valley of the Desperately Direct*, at least at the outset, in which you propose in a calm voice and serene manner the idea of setting a weekly schedule for sexual encounters.

For some of you, this schedule may include a few to even several encounters a week, but I doubt it…mostly because you are reading this guide. This proposed schedule probably includes a once – *maybe* twice – a week appointment to have sex. There will probably be two to three days in between these appointments, so as not to overtax your partner and to give you some well-spaced satisfaction with him or her during the week. A likely proposed schedule could include sex on Sundays and Wednesdays, or Tuesdays and Saturdays.

It is essential to bring up the subject of the weekly schedule when you feel calm and not very desperate, which is probably directly after a Poke-n-Stay situation. While relaxing in the Afterglow of a satisfactory sexual experience, consider saying something like, "Hey, I was thinking…what do you think about setting up a schedule for sex?"

This could go one of two ways: A) your partner is amenable to the idea and continues the conversation or B) your partner feels that sex should be passionate and spontaneous and not set into a schedule like something as unromantic as a teeth

cleaning. If the response is A, then great, keep

going. If the response is B), then great, keep going.

You didn't come this far just to roll over and give

up.

Regardless of the response, continue the

conversation with, "Great! I was thinking twice a

week." Propose two days during the week that you

can put sex on the calendar. Be sure to include a

weekend day, as presumably there is a higher chance

for sleeping in and a larger chunk of the day for

gettin' it on. Keep in mind that you might have to

propose once a week at first; if this is the case,

definitely go with a weekend.

Since you have spearheaded the idea of

putting sex days on the calendar, it is essential to

actually make notes on the calendar to set the appointments in stone. Whether the calendar is one of those traditional flip-the-month kinds or a shared Google calendar, schedule in the sex days to repeat, with an end date of "Never." Set those Sex Day appointments with a child's confidence that Santa is real.

Because nothing is private anymore, whether your calendar is in print or online, you may need to make a code for Sex Day. Since you have presumably created code words ala *Talk Dirty to Me* and *Time is of the Essence*, using your specialized phrases shouldn't be a problem.

On Sex Day

Putting Sex Days on the calendar isn't like using a Ronco Rotisserie. Ron Popeil isn't sitting at your bedside yelling, "Set it and forget it!"

You've done the first part, my friend. Now it is time to keep the appointment.

The series of friendly reminders begin on the morning of Sex Day. As your partner awakens, make a declaration like, "Good morning! It's Sex Day! Don't forget…" with a smile may be all you need to keep the appointment, even if he or she groans or rolls his or her eyes. Stay strong!

Follow the clock to remind your partner of Sex Day, sending Google invites and planning friendly notices at lunchtime and/or during dinner. If many cues are needed – and you know your partner better than anyone – then pretend like your partner is a toddler who needs to eat every few hours. Helpful statements may include:

- "We're on, right?"
- "We're good to go for tonight, yes?"
- "Don't forget, it's Sex Day."
- "What time do you want to play hide the sausage?"
- "When can I ride the sausage pony?"

There are, in fact, several sentences that could incorporate the word "sausage" in the method of double entendre. In this case, consider serving sausage for breakfast and/or dinner to make it a theme. If sausage itself is a problem, go with other suggestively shaped foods, such as bananas, eggplant, cucumbers, long sweet potatoes, salami, and hot dogs. Taken together, all of these could make quite a balanced meal.

If friendly or gentle reminders aren't doing the job, consider taking the intensity up a notch. Personally, I like to use more direct statements or questions, like:

- "Exactly what time can we do it?"
  And
- "Don't think you are going to get out of this."

Granted, these two statements may not be the optimal ways to keep your partner committed to Sex Day. However, these directly ribald statements may occur on those tougher days. Like when the teenager in the house has done nothing but argue and roll his eyes at everything you say. Or when the toddler managed somehow to poop outside of the toilet for the third time. Perhaps there is no wine or chocolate in the house, and you can't remember the last time you used the bathroom without the attention of the children and the dog. And the only touching you have experienced was when the checker handed over your change at the grocery store.

Fortunately, not everything has to be perfect for Sex Day. After all, this special appointment is on the calendar primarily because so many days are chaotic and not "ideal" for sexual encounters. If they should want to cancel Sex Day, partners need to keep in mind that sex is, in fact, an enjoyable activity. This is not an appointment to do the taxes or scrub the bathroom or buy a car or clean out a human-sized birdcage. This is sex, and it doesn't have to be fancy. Partners may want to refer to *Time is of the Essence* to make the most of their energy levels and available time.

Like a condom, setting and keeping Sex Day appointments can ensure that partners directly communicate their needs without unintended lasting consequences besides what is desired, which is an enjoyable sexual encounter.

Technique #7: Put On Notice

The beginning of the end on the *Spectrum of Sexual Persuasion*, this method is one of the most assertive strategies involving trying to get sex from your mate. This strategy is used most during periods of extreme stress or fatigue, like family vacations or the holidays.

Putting someone "On Notice" is more of a legal or formal term, not to be taken lightly. Being put On Notice was a segment on The Colbert Report, which was the second stage in being called out for a transgression. Once Stephen Colbert put something or someone On Notice, they had 60 days

61

to appear on the show and apologize. If they refused to appear, the offenders were moved to the "Dead to Me" board. The objects and people who were on Stephen Colbert's "On Notice" board included Distractions, Grizzly Bears, Barbra Streisand, Forgiveness, Michael Adams, and Pant Cuffs. These were the items that angered Colbert the most.

Like Colbert, individuals who put their partners On Notice are at the height of frustration and are in desperate need. This strategy is not a gentle reminder, but a stern warning in a vaguely threatening manner, a way of telling your partner that he or she has been warned that sexual acts of a form meeting your desires are necessary as soon as possible.

Putting your partner On Notice is a form of the standard, tried and true ultimatum, stating the need, a specific period of time for fulfillment, and a threat in case the action is not brought to completion. The Put On Notice strategy could begin with this sentence:

"You are put on notice that I need sex tonight, or..."

First, the structure of this On Notice is sound, in that the need is clear and there is a definite due date. The "or" at the end signifies a threat, which begs the question: Or what?

Choosing the Threat

Including a threat might seem distasteful, but remember that this strategy is meant to induce guilt and should be used in only the most desperate circumstances.

Threats to add to the Put On Notice strategy will vary from couple to couple, but might include:

- Going on strike. Choose something that your partner really cares about. Clean dishes? Cooked meals? That you take showers or get dressed? Then go on strike with one or more of those things.

- Taking something away. Granted, taking away sex won't work here. But taking away the remote to the TV would, and there are a lot of hiding places in the house. In fact, when your partner tries to find the TV remote, you could say that it is in your pants, along with the party he or she is now invited to attend.

- Disappearing for a while. Nobody can miss you if you never leave, even if it is only for an afternoon. Consider going somewhere overnight, leaving your partner to take care of everything without you. Your absence may cause more than his or her heart to grow warmer.

- Crying. Many people do not like to see others crying. Why do you think little kids use this strategy so much to get what they want? Because it can be very effective, even when you are an adult.

- The Silent Treatment. Granted, this could work against you if you enjoy talking and your partner doesn't enjoy listening, but it is a way to help your partner miss you without having to actually go anywhere.

These are just a few simple suggestions that could be incorporated, but you know your partner better than anyone else – the more creative you can be, the better.

The Importance of the Follow-Through

Putting someone On Notice requires follow through when it comes to the threat, or your partner will not believe you in the future. Action is essential at this point on the spectrum. For example, consider for a moment not paying your electricity bill. What will eventually happen? If you don't pay your bill, the electric company will shut off your service.

Be the electric company, and make good on your consequences. You will be fueled by sexual frustration, so making good on your threat shouldn't be a problem.

Just be sure to get 'er done – if you threaten to cry and are still refused sex when putting a partner on notice, you had best work up some tears, and make it good.

Using This Strategy's Back Door

There is another slightly more acceptable way to use the Put On Notice strategy, and that is handling the entire exchange from the possible perspective of your partner. In other words, if you scratch his or her back (perhaps literally), then he or she will mostly likely scratch yours in return.

Perhaps there is something in your sexual encounters that you have been holding back or not willing to try. This could be the leverage you need to get the sex that you want.

A rephrase of the Put On Notice could go something like this:

"You are put on notice that I need sex tonight, AND I am willing to try such-and-so..." And you could say this while whipping out the fuzzy handcuffs and silk blindfold.

Notice the "and" that is currently where the "or" used to be. Since you are willing to make a trade of sorts, a threat may no longer be necessary. Your willingness to trade may only be limited by your imagination, as you could also try role play, accouterments, fun with edibles, or different positions. You know best what your partner might want in trade.

Considered less than ideal, putting your partner "On Notice" could be the strategy you need to achieve the sexual satisfaction you desire.

Technique #8: Master of Your Fate

If you want something done right, you should do it yourself.

While a popular saying for many activities, this simply does not apply to sex. When it comes to sex, "doing it yourself" can leave something to be desired. If we should indeed "do it ourselves" for maximum pleasure, there would not be nearly as many sex-based accessories available for sale.

While it isn't ideal approach sex as a Do-It-Yourself project, it may become necessary. Life happens, and even partners who willing schedule and usually keep Sex Day appointments can find themselves stranded in sexual desperation.

Hence, the sex accouterments; or, as they are more widely called, sex "toys." There are many different kinds of "toys" for individuals at every stage of desperation and experience. While generally supportive of the idea of sex "toys," this author takes issue with the term "toys" when it comes to these valuable and useful tools.

These accouterments are not casual playthings that can be tossed aside when a noisier or shinier bauble comes along. These sexual accessories are diligently applied to complete a necessary task, many times when the user is in desperate need.

The word "toys" implies a certain glibness of attitude, as if we are really only interested in the boxes these tools arrived in, like a cat or a toddler at Christmas. For the purposes of this guide, these tools will not be called toys; they are called Sex Necessities. As in, they are necessary for our sanity when one or more of the seduction strategies set forth in this guide fails to work.

The Master of Your Fate

It is sometimes necessary to be the Master of Your Fate when you are in need of sexual satisfaction but can't seem to convince your mate to join in the fun. While mastering your fate the old-fashioned way is time-tested and ultimately pleasurable, there are times when a little battery-powered help is a welcome addition to this exercise in self-care.

Discomfort can arise, however, from the noisy nature of many of the Sex Necessities on the market, especially for women. Your mate may be a really light sleeper, and the buzzing accompanying your solo trysts may give you away. However, this development can work in your favor when trying to get sex from your mate. He or she may take notice of your activities without you having to say a word.

There are also times when conversation is necessary in order to get the sexual satisfaction we need. And sometimes these "conversations" are really thinly-veiled threats.

Making Threats with Sex Necessities

The use of threats to try and achieve sexual intimacy and satisfaction with your partner requires careful consideration. Threats should never be intended to harm another person. This can be a fine line on which to balance, so this author urges readers to think really carefully before setting up a threat to try and get sex.

The threat involving being the Master of Your Fate – with or without Sex Necessities –must focus on the fun that your partner will miss out on by not participating.

For example, a threat that the author finds both useful and harmless includes conversation involving this sentence: "Fine, if you're not going to have sex with me, I'll do it myself!"

The use of this sentence could result in one of three scenarios:

- Your partner feels sorry for you and decides to show some mercy by giving you the sexual satisfaction you need. This is, of course, the most ideal situation.

- Your partner's eyes light up in anticipation, and you continue the delicate conversation involving this new bedroom activity that your partner may not have considered.

- Your partner shrugs, leaves the room, and you decide whether or not to make good on your statement. Since you have the alone time and the Sex Necessities, you may as well imbibe. Hey, it's better

than nothin'!

Will You Go Blind?

Simply put, there is nothing to lose by being

the Master of Your Fate.

First, you won't go blind. As a child, I heard

the well-worn rumor that if I spent time being the

Master of My Fate, then I would be struck blind. If

that was the case, we would all be blind.

Second, it's free. This activity – without Sex

Necessities, of course – literally costs no money.

Third, it's easy. (Unless you're a dude, then

it's hard. That's what she said. See what I did

there?) Seriously, though, this activity isn't like

cleaning the bathroom or going for a run or making

dinner. You aren't going to want to poke your eyes

out. This is actually a really nice way to spend 20 minutes or more, depending on how much time you have.

Fourth, there are no diseases associated with this activity. You won't be infected by anything except a sense of relief and some naturally-occurring dopamine.

And last but certainly not least, you need to know your own body. If you don't know what's down there, how are you supposed to boss someone else regarding what methods you prefer? (And by "boss," I mean "gently direct.")

While the old adage, "If you want something done right, you should do it yourself" may not apply to sexual satisfaction, this method can be used in order to interest your partner and hopefully help you

get the sex that you need.

Technique #9: Under Threat of Death

The last and most guilt-driven of the strategies to get sex from your mate involves the threat of death. However – and this is *extremely* important – you are *not* threatening the other person with death. Threatening someone else with death in order to have sex lacks manners. There is no room for that kind of behavior in this guide.

Instead, you are guilting your partner with the idea of your own possible death.

Let's face it, death is the inevitable end for each of us. While considering the end of our lives is unpleasant, there is a way to use this line of thinking in order to get the sex that we need from our mates.

This strategy is best used after a sad event, such as watching a movie that made you both tear up a little, or the death of a neighbor's pet, or the birth of a baby (preferably not from your loins). Nothing reminds you of your own mortality like seeing a brand new baby.

This strategy requires setting the scene. While not necessarily romantic, the lights need to be turned down so that darkness can seep in around the edges a little bit. Employ soft lighting, maybe consider burning some candles. Turn off any music, television, or games that may distract your partner from thoughts of imminent death and sadness. Take your partner in your arms and snuggle together in the peace and quiet.

This is a great time to remind your partner of lost opportunities and abandoned dreams, followed by the conversation involving which one of your may die before the other one. Smooth your partner's hair back and gently whisper, "If I died tomorrow, you would be really sad that you didn't have sex with me right now."

Follow this statement up with gentle kisses, hopefully stemming the tide of any indignation that may arise. Keep your overall goal in mind, shoving down any residual discomfort from employing this strategy.

You will both die someday.

You need sex from your mate.

You are clearly desperate.

Keep fighting the good fight!

Acknowledgements

A book like this is a ton of fun to write. I appreciate my husband for telling me from the beginning that he did not wish to be featured in this work of art. I loved being able to write without worrying about embarrassing anyone else but myself. Clearly, I have no shame.

I also want to think my early and later readers of this project, including Lisa Mills, Jone MacColloch, Julia Shaw, Melissa Flickinger, Paul Fankhauser, Jen Erskine, Janice Erickson, Christine Draper, Aaron Barnes, Nadeen Wilson, Heather

Michet, Stephanie Winston, and Dana Campbell –
thank you for your feedback, edits, and support.
Special thanks go to Charlotte Kammer, who
listened to my sexual-lack-of-conquest stories day
after day; she told me to immediately begin writing
them down and helped create the title for this
amazing work of nonfiction. Many thanks to Shari
Ryan at Mad Hat Books for help with the cover.

No sense of pride or ego was harmed in the creation of this book.

About the Author

Kelly Wilson is an author and comedian who entertains and inspires with stories of humor, healing, and hope. She is the author of *Live Cheap and Free* and *Don't Punch People in the Junk*. Her latest book, *Caskets From Costco*, is a finalist in the 18th annual Foreword Reviews' INDIEFAB Book of the Year Awards and has also been chosen as a finalist in the 10th annual National Indie Excellence Book Awards.

As a survivor of childhood sexual abuse, Kelly writes and speaks about finding hope in the process of recovery. Through both stand-up and improv comedy, she brings laughter to audiences of all ages using a wide range of subject matter, including silly songs, parenting stories, and jokes and anecdotes revolving around mental health issues.

Kelly Wilson currently writes for a living and lives with her Magically Delicious husband, junk-punching children, dog, cat, and stereotypical minivan in Portland, Oregon. Read more about her at www.wilsonwrites.com.